FORGOTTEN YOUTH

Homeless Youth

Cherese Cartlidge

ReferencePoint Press®

San Diego, CA

© 2017 ReferencePoint Press, Inc.
Printed in the United States

For more information, contact:
ReferencePoint Press, Inc.
PO Box 27779
San Diego, CA 92198
www.ReferencePointPress.com

LIBRARY OF CONGRESS CATALOGING-IN-PUBLICATION DATA

Name: Cartlidge, Cherese, author.
Title: Homeless youth / by Cherese Cartlidge.
Description: San Diego, CA : ReferencePoint Press, Inc., 2017. | Series:
    Forgotten youth | Includes bibliographical references and index.
Identifiers: LCCN 2016004055 | ISBN 9781601529787 (hardback)
Subjects: LCSH: Homeless youth--United States--Juvenile literature. |
    Homelessness--United States--Juvenile literature.
Classification: LCC HV4505 .C337 2017 | DDC 362.7/756920973--dc23
LC record available at http://lccn.loc.gov/2016004055

Contents

Kids Living in the Shadows

William's life is very different from that of most other students at his New York City high school. He does not have a smartphone or an iPod. He does not have athletic gear, a pet, or even family photos. In fact, William does not have many possessions at all. And he is never able to keep his belongings for longer than about a year, because he and his mother move so often. The two of them have been homeless since William was three years old, when they were forced to leave the house they shared with his grandfather. Over the years, they frequently moved from one homeless shelter to another or stayed temporarily in the home of friends or relatives. But William and his mother never allowed themselves to become too settled in any one place, because they knew they would likely have to move again soon.

Life in the shelters for William and his mother was hectic and strict: There were frequent room checks and fire drills, and residents had to sign in and out. There were also limits on how often residents could leave the shelter. "We had very little freedom," says William, who describes the shelter as feeling "like an asylum."[1] By the time William was in high school, his mother was able to find a job. Thanks to a transitional housing program, the two of them now live in a small apartment where they pay rent on a sliding scale based on his mother's income. But people are allowed to stay in housing programs like this for a limited time—usually only a few months. So William knows they will soon have to move yet again. In the meantime, they live in constant fear of not being able to pay the rent and of being evicted. Anytime they get behind on the rent, William worries they will wind up back in a shelter or out on the streets.

Invisible Kids

William is one of the more than twenty-two thousand homeless youth in New York City. There are thousands more homeless children and teens in cities across the country. Yet homeless youth are often a forgotten group, one that most people are not even aware exists. The National Coalition for the Homeless (NCH) estimates that as many as 3.5 million people experience homelessness each year in the United States. Most of these are adults, and many of those suffer from some sort of mental illness. They sleep in parks or on downtown sidewalks, push shopping carts piled high with found objects, stand at intersections with signs asking for money, or wander aimlessly on skid rows, unshaven and clad in multiple layers of dirty clothing. This is the face of homelessness in America that most people know. Almost invisible are the more than 2 million young people who, either alone or with their families, have no place to call home.

One reason homeless youth may be overlooked is that most of them just look like other kids their age. This was the case with one fifteen-year-old girl who visited Randy Christensen, a pediatrician who specializes in treating homeless children. He explains, "She was not sleeping in doorways, and if you saw her at a bus stop, you would think she was just another girl, a little heavy and probably poor. You wouldn't know she had no real home."[2] Indeed, many homeless youth look and act no differently than any other kid walking on the street or down a hallway at school. Many of them earn high grades or play sports at school, giving every appearance of being "normal." One writer who profiled a homeless family in Scholastic's *Storyworks* magazine says, "You may see a homeless person every day and have no idea."[3]

> "They spend their days in school, their nights in shelters. They are seen only in glimpses."[4]
>
> —Andrea Elliott, an investigative reporter with the *New York Times.*

More often than not, homeless youth look no different from their peers. This is one reason they are easily overlooked.

Hidden Youth

Another reason homeless youth often go unnoticed is that many of them keep out of sight. As Andrea Elliott, an investigative reporter with the *New York Times*, explains, "They spend their days in school, their nights in shelters. They are seen only in glimpses."[4]

In addition, many homeless youth hide the fact that they are homeless, whether out of pride, fear, or shame. Maria Fabian, who was homeless while in high school, worked hard to hide her situation from others because she worried about what people at her school would think of her if they knew the truth. "It took me a long time to realize that my story is not all that unique," says Fabian. "It's a good bet that there are homeless youth in the shadows of every school in our country."[5]

For these and myriad other reasons, the thousands of homeless youth who exist in communities all across the United States remain invisible to the public eye. Yet they exist in every city and every state in this nation. The trauma homeless kids undergo at such a young age can leave scars that affect them the rest of their lives.

Chapter 1

A Vulnerable Population

For millions of people in the United States who have no permanent residence, homelessness is a traumatic experience. It is especially wrenching for children and teens—who need stability in order to thrive—to find themselves without the comfort and security of having a home. Being homeless at such a vulnerable stage in their lives has many consequences for youth, both in the short term and the long term.

What Does It Mean to Be Homeless?

When people hear the word *homeless*, particular images often come to mind. One image is of a person who lives on the street—sleeping in public parks, in doorways, or under bridges. And when they think of homeless youth, many people probably picture teens who have run away from home and find themselves alone with nowhere to go. Both of these situations exist, to be sure. But there are many circumstances in which a person can be considered homeless.

First of all, to be homeless does not necessarily mean to be without shelter. Homeless people may indeed sleep outside, seeking shelter under a porch, in a dumpster, or even inside a cardboard box. But the US Department of Housing and Urban Development (HUD) also defines individuals as homeless if they live in a homeless assistance program, such as an emergency shelter or transitional housing. These "sheltered homeless" may also live in places that are not meant for human habitation, including a car or abandoned building. People who couch surf—staying a night or two on the couch of a friend or relative before moving on to the next couch—are also considered homeless by HUD, as are families that move into the apartment or home of others because of economic hardship.

Some people are homeless temporarily, such as those who are displaced by a natural disaster; often people in these circumstances find a new home in a relatively short time. Others are homeless long term. HUD considers a person to be chronically homeless if he or she has been continuously homeless for one year or longer or has experienced homelessness at least four times in the past three years.

Causes of Youth Homelessness

Whatever form their homelessness takes, a variety of factors can lead to youth becoming homeless. Many of these are economic. Some youth become homeless after a parent loses a job and gets behind on the rent or mortgage, which can lead to being evicted from the home. Other kids may have been born to parents who were homeless. The Great Recession of 2007–2009 continues to be a factor in homelessness. Bruce Lesley, president of the advocacy group First Focus Campaign for Children, points out that during any recession, families with children tend to be the first to fall into poverty. In addition, says Lesley, "Kids are the last to recover. Because this recession was because of housing, it's been particularly bad for kids."[6]

For many families who are still struggling to recover from the effects of the Great Recession, affordable housing remains out of reach. Lower-income families often must spend a large proportion of their income on their rent, which puts them at risk of homelessness. One indication of this struggle is the number of people who live doubled up with family and friends. The National Alliance to End Homelessness (NAEH) reports that the number of people in this living situation has increased 67 percent since 2007. Living doubled up puts people and families in a precarious situation, because often they are sharing living quarters without legally being on any lease, which makes them vulnerable to being kicked out. The NAEH considers living doubled up to be a huge risk factor for becoming homeless. In fact, this living situation often represents the final desperate attempt to keep a roof over their heads for people who eventually become homeless.

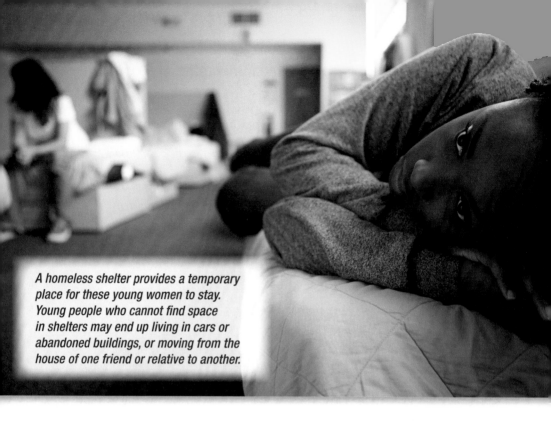

A homeless shelter provides a temporary place for these young women to stay. Young people who cannot find space in shelters may end up living in cars or abandoned buildings, or moving from the house of one friend or relative to another.

Other causes of homelessness stem from individual or family dysfunction. Some youth may become homeless after their parents divorce or after the death of a parent. Many homeless youth have parents with drug or alcohol addictions or mental health issues such as depression or schizophrenia. Some homeless kids have substance abuse or mental health problems themselves. Others experience homelessness because one or more parent is in jail. Pediatrician Randy Christensen, who provides health care to homeless youth, says, "I often saw kids who were homeless because their families were fragmented, destitute, traveling from one crime-ridden apartment to another, ravaged by domestic violence and drug abuse."[7]

Some teens wind up homeless after running away from neglect, family conflict, or abuse. Others have been kicked out of their home due to drug or alcohol problems, brushes with the law, getting pregnant, or coming out to their parents, among other reasons. These kids are sometimes called "throwaways"—kids who have been thrown out by their families. One homeless teen girl explains how her father kicked her out of the house by driving her away from home and abandoning her: "My dad dropped me off at a dumpster. He told me don't even think about coming back home."[8] And a mentally challenged teen named Donald wound up homeless after his physically abusive father put him on a bus from Alabama to Arizona, with a fictitious address for a family member who did not exist.

How Many Homeless Youth Are There?

It is not known for certain how many children and teens are homeless in the United States. Estimates of the number of homeless kids age eighteen and younger in the nation vary widely. There are a number of reasons for this. One is that many homeless youth who are on their own try to hide from authorities. They may have run away from an abusive home, for example, and are fearful of being returned to their parents or the foster care system. Homeless youth who are mistrustful of others tend not to interact with standard homeless assistance programs or government agencies. In addition, solutions for homelessness in general are often not applicable to minors—they are ineligible to rent an apartment, for example, and many homeless shelters either do not take unaccompanied youth or have a limited number of beds for them. For these reasons, it is difficult to get an accurate picture of the number of homeless kids.

Nevertheless, HUD conducts an annual count each January of the number of homeless people who live in shelters or on the street in communities across the nation. These are known as point-in-time counts. The NAEH notes that it is fairly easy to count the number of youths living in shelters, but it is extremely difficult to get an accurate count of the number of kids who

"I often saw kids who were homeless because their families were fragmented, destitute, traveling from one crime-ridden apartment to another, ravaged by domestic violence and drug abuse."[7]

—Pediatrician Randy Christensen, who provides health care to homeless youth.

Becoming Homeless

There are many factors that can lead to a youth experiencing homelessness. The majority of homeless kids live with one or more family members. Often they become homeless when their parents are no longer able to afford the rent or house payment. This was the case with Gina Cooper and her twelve-year-old son, Dante Walton. Cooper had a low-wage job that paid less than ten dollars an hour. She and her son lived in San Francisco, where housing costs are very high, and Cooper struggled to pay her rent. In 2012 she was so far behind that she and her son were evicted. For the next several months, the two of them stayed a night or two with friends or relatives, sleeping in spare bedrooms or on the floor or living room couch, before moving on to their next temporary stay.

Eventually, Cooper and her son were able to find space in a homeless shelter. They stayed in the shelter for several months while she continued working and saving up for a home of their own. But their stressful and uncertain existence took its toll on Walton, who was in middle school at the time. "It was a painful time for my son," Cooper recalls. "On the way to school, he would be crying, 'I hate this.'" After five months, Cooper saved enough money to rent a small house south of San Francisco.

Quoted in David Crary and Lisa Leff, "Number of Homeless Children in America Surges to All-Time High: Report," *Huffington Post*, November 17, 2014. www.huffingtonpost.com.

live on the streets. "Often they're invisible, either by intention or by accident,"[9] says the NAEH. In addition, unaccompanied, unsheltered homeless kids tend to hang out in different places and at different times than homeless adults, and they may be unwilling to admit that they are homeless. "To do a good street count, you have to know where to look,"[10] explains the NAEH. Despite these flaws, HUD's annual point-in-time counts provide a fairly reliable snapshot of the number of homeless youth in America.

According to HUD's latest point-in-time count, there were nearly six hundred thousand homeless people in the United

States on a single night in January 2015. Author Gary Levine, who has worked with homeless children and families, states, "For purposes of perspective, consider that the Amalie Arena, home of the Tampa Bay Lightning, has a seating capacity of 20,500. It would require nearly 30 such arenas to house that evening's homeless community."[11] Yet this figure represents only the number of people who were homeless at the time of the count. Thousands of others were homeless at different points throughout the year and for varying lengths of time. According to the NCH, up to 3.5 million people experience homelessness at some point each year. Because of the difficulties involved in locating and identifying them, estimates of the total number of youth age eighteen and under who experience homelessness each year in the United States vary. The National Association for the Education of Homeless Children and Youth reports that 1,360,747 homeless students were enrolled in US public schools in the 2013–2014 school year. But that number only reflects school-age children who were enrolled in school. The total number of kids age eighteen and under who experience homelessness each year is much higher—as many as 2.5 million, according to the National Center on Family Homelessness (NCFH).

Even more sobering is the fact that not all of these 2.5 million homeless children have a parent or other family member to look out for them. The US Department of Education (DOE) estimates about 6 percent of homeless students are unaccompanied, whereas HUD places that estimate at 7.8 percent. That means anywhere from about forty-five thousand to eighty-one thousand homeless youth live completely on their own.

Where Is the Problem the Worst?

There are homeless youth age eighteen and younger in cities and towns in every state in the nation. But some places have a higher prevalence than others. In 2015 there were 7,260 homeless people in Hawaii, which gave the state the highest homeless rate per capita of any state in the nation. Hawaii's homeless rate was followed closely by that of New York and Nevada. However, for sheer numbers, it should come as no surprise that the most populous

The Population of Homeless Young People Living on Their Own

Experts estimate that more than 2 million kids face a period of homelessness in the United States each year. Some of these young people are accompanied by family members; others (described as unaccompanied) live on their own. Accurate counts of homeless youth are hard to come by, partly because those who live on their own tend to hide from public view. In its 2015 report, the National Alliance to End Homelessness provides a snapshot of the unaccompanied children and youth homeless population (which includes young people up to age twenty-four). The numbers show what percentage of the homeless population they represented in each state in 2014.

Percentage of homeless people who are unaccompanied children and youth, 2014

Legend:
- 0% to 5%
- 5% to 10%
- 10% to 15%
- More than 15%

Source: National Alliance to End Homelessness, *The State of Homelessness in America 2015*. Washington, DC: National Alliance to End Homelessness, 2015, p. 31. www.endhomelessness.org.

state, California, has the largest number of homeless people, as well as the largest number of homeless kids. In 2015 the state reported it had more than 310,000 homeless children, almost one-fourth of the national total. The states with the next-highest numbers of homeless children were New York, Texas, Florida, Illinois, Michigan, Georgia, Washington, Kentucky, and Missouri, in that order. California is also the state with the highest number of unaccompanied homeless youth under age eighteen—more than 1,780 in 2014. Other states with a high number of unaccompanied homeless youth include Florida, with 1,230, and Nevada, with 773.

Whether they are on their own or living with family, homeless kids tend to be most prevalent in large urban areas. For example, Chicago, Illinois, and San Diego, California, each had more than twenty-two thousand homeless students during the 2014–2015 school year. And New York City, the nation's largest city, has more than forty-five thousand homeless families with children. According to HUD, five major cities—Los Angeles, San Francisco, and San Jose, all in California; Las Vegas, Nevada; and New York City—account for about one-fourth of all unaccompanied homeless youth in the nation. In fact, Los Angeles is considered the nation's "homeless capital" because of the large number of people who live on the streets there—an estimated forty-six thousand in 2015.

Emotional Effects of Homelessness

No matter where homeless youth are located, the effects of homelessness on them can be especially devastating. Homelessness can lead to an array of emotional and social consequences. Psychological effects of homelessness on youth include low self-esteem, depression, and anxiety. Homeless teens are more likely to be depressed and suicidal than teens from a stable, permanent home. They are also more likely to abuse alcohol and other substances. In one survey conducted in the early 2000s by a health care team in Phoenix, Arizona, 66 percent of homeless teens reported they were depressed, 44 percent said they had engaged in self-harm with thoughts of suicide in the previous six months, and 82 percent indicated they were substance abusers.

Another emotional effect of homelessness on kids is feelings of embarrassment or shame over their situation. Many kids who feel ashamed of being homeless try to hide their situation from others. These feelings can be compounded by public attitudes toward the homeless. One eleven-year-old homeless girl, Dasani, worked hard to keep the fact that she lived in a homeless shelter a secret from others. She and her siblings would hang out at a nearby playground after school until the other children were gone, biding their time until they could slip into the shelter unseen. If others noticed them going in or out of the shelter, she and her siblings would be called "shelter boogies"[12] by the other kids—a term that deeply embarrassed Dasani.

One particularly difficult effect of homelessness on youth is the problem of making and maintaining friendships. Feelings of shame can play a role in this. Teen Kevin Liu and his family were homeless for three years and stayed in a shelter in New York City. According to Liu, he dreaded when his classmates asked him where he lived. He would change the subject, give vague replies, or even lie to his friends. "I felt like I could never truly be myself and open up to my friends because I carried around this secret,"[13] he says.

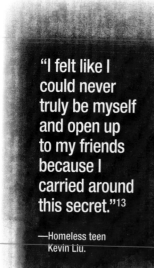

"I felt like I could never truly be myself and open up to my friends because I carried around this secret."[13]

—Homeless teen Kevin Liu.

Another factor that makes it difficult for homeless kids to have friends is that they may move around a lot. Evan Goehring and his mother were homeless while he was a teen. "When I was growing up, I never really had true friends because of how much I moved,"[14] he said. Because of the frequent moves, he changed schools virtually every year.

Social isolation is a frequent result of homelessness, regardless of the young person's particular living situation. Whether they live in a shelter, sleep in a car, or move from one house to the next, few homeless young people manage to create lasting relationships with peers. Newspaper columnist Ann Brenoff points out, "You can't have kids over to play or have

Homeless teens may turn to alcohol and other substances in hopes of escaping the stressful conditions of their lives. Depression and suicidal thoughts are also common among homeless youth.

a friend sleep over if your home is the car."[15] And for homeless youth who live on their own on the streets, without family or shelter, life can be extremely isolating.

Long-Term Consequences

Homeless kids face many challenges to their health and well-being that can lead to an array of long-term consequences. For example, homeless youth are more likely to get sick than kids who have a home—according to the Brookings Institution, they get sick four times as often. Those who live in a poor environment— such as a run-down homeless shelter, an abandoned building, or on the streets—may be exposed to unclean conditions that contribute to health issues. And because their immune systems may be worn down by factors such as poor nutrition or stress, it may take them longer to recover from a simple illness such as a cold. In addition, homeless kids have a higher risk of contracting serious illnesses such as hepatitis C. They are also more likely to be the victims of violence, become sexually active at a young age,

Living Doubled Up

Seventeen-year-old Juan lives doubled up in a two-bedroom apartment in Los Angeles with eight other family members because his mother cannot afford rent on a place of their own. His grandmother, grandfather, and an uncle sleep in the small, cramped living room. An aunt and teenage cousin live in one bedroom. Juan shares the other bedroom with his mother and his younger brother and sister; the floor of the bedroom is constantly strewn with toys and clothes. Juan sleeps in the closet, where his bed takes up most of the available space and a shelf above his head serves as his dresser. He describes what it is like to live doubled up in a small apartment:

> It's kinda difficult with so many people, sometimes you do things and they don't like it, like when my brother listens to music, my aunt starts complaining cause she don't like that kind of music that my brother listens to, so she's complaining about it and all of a sudden my grandpa is complaining cause he say we're not organized, like we all be leaving a big mess. So I try my best to keep everything organized and not to bother them. . . . It's kinda hard because you lose a lot of things that you are not allowed to do no more, like some noises because the neighbors might complain about it. Sometimes my sister runs, she start running around the apartment, the lady downstairs be complaining all the time.

Quoted in Ronald E. Hallett, *Educational Experiences of Hidden Homeless Teenagers*. New York: Routledge, 2012, pp. 56, 63–64.

be sexually abused, or engage in prostitution than are kids from a stable home.

In addition to health issues, a number of other factors can contribute to long-term problems for homeless kids. According to the NCFH, homeless kids experience emotional and behavioral problems at three times the rate of kids who are not homeless. The disruptions they experience in their lives make it more likely they will do poorly in school and eventually drop out. A poor education can lower their earning potential as adults. They are more likely to be unemployed and to be incarcerated as adults. And according to the Brookings Institution, homeless kids are five times more likely than their peers to become homeless as adults.

All of these factors can affect homeless kids for the rest of their lives. As *New York Times* reporter Andrea Elliott explains, "With each passing month, they slip further back in every category known to predict long-term well-being. They are less likely to graduate from the schools that anchor them, and more likely to end up like their parents, their lives circumscribed by teenage pregnancy or shortened by crime and illness."[16]

Homeless youth are at an incredible disadvantage as they move through life, and they may suffer long-term consequences well into their adulthood. As the NCFH explains in its report, *America's Youngest Outcasts*:

> Children experiencing homelessness are among the most invisible and neglected individuals in our nation. Despite their ever-growing number, homeless children have no voice and no constituency. Without a bed to call their own, they have lost safety, privacy, and the comforts of home, as well as friends, pets, possessions, reassuring routines, and community. These losses combine to create a life-altering experience that inflicts profound and lasting scars.[17]

"When I was growing up, I never really had true friends because of how much I moved."[14]

—Homeless teen Evan Goehring.

Chapter 2

Finding Food and Shelter

Many homeless youth have a hard time finding a suitable place to sleep and enough food to eat. This is true whether they are on their own or living with family. There are different types of homeless shelters, but not all homeless kids live in a shelter; in fact, some do not have a roof over their heads at all. And many homeless kids face hunger on a daily basis. Whatever their particular circumstances, being without a permanent home is a traumatic and devastating situation for young people.

Types of Shelters

There are a variety of settings that can be considered a form of homeless shelter, and some serve different populations of homeless people. Shelters may be specifically for adults without kids, adults or families with kids, victims of domestic violence, gay and transgender people, or youth on their own. Homeless shelters vary in terms of their physical layout. Some shelters consist of a large barracks-style room in which many individuals and families share the same sleeping, bathing, and eating areas. In other shelters, each family has its own room and either a private or a communal bathroom.

Homeless shelters also vary as to how long people can stay; some are short term and others long term. Temporary shelters include emergency shelters such as those that serve victims of domestic violence or sexual abuse. These are temporary havens where people can stay for one or two nights. Most operate on a first-come, first-served basis and have limited hours they are open, as well as curfews. One example is the First Friendship Family Shelter in San Francisco, open from 3:00 p.m. to 7:00

a.m. every night of the year. An adult must call between noon and 2:00 p.m. to reserve a space for the family for the night; one adult must arrive by 6:00 p.m. to claim the slot or the reservation is canceled, and the remaining family members must arrive by 8:00 p.m. This is an emergency family shelter, where families are allowed to stay only one night.

Children under eighteen are not allowed to reserve space for the family at the First Friendship Family Shelter or to enter the shelter without an adult. So it is not an option for kids who are on their own. But there are emergency shelters specifically for youth, usually known as safe houses. These serve homeless kids under age eighteen who are in need of immediate shelter, but kids can only stay for a few nights. A longer-term option for homeless kids on their own would be a youth shelter, which is a shelter specifically for kids under age eighteen.

The most common situation for a homeless child or teen, however, is a family homeless shelter. Unlike emergency shelters, which provide a place to sleep at night but require people to stay elsewhere during the day, a long-term homeless shelter allows families to live there day and night—some for months at a time. In addition, such shelters often limit how often or how long people can be away from the shelter; space is limited, so the rooms in these shelters must go to those who truly have no place else to stay.

It is common for homeless families to progress through the various levels of shelters from temporary emergency shelters, to long-term family shelters, and then into a transitional living program. Such programs usually help people live in their own apartment, either by providing a subsidy to help pay the rent or allowing people to pay rent on a sliding scale based on their income. There are transitional living programs in communities throughout the nation. The length of time people are allowed to stay varies, depending on the program; people can stay anywhere from six or seven months up to a year or two.

On the Streets

Although most homeless people find space in some type of shelter, some have no shelter to speak of. According to the NAEH,

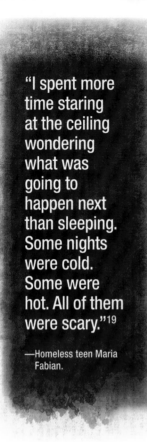

"I spent more time staring at the ceiling wondering what was going to happen next than sleeping. Some nights were cold. Some were hot. All of them were scary."[19]

—Homeless teen Maria Fabian.

about 31 percent of homeless people are unsheltered—either living on the streets or in a place that is unfit for human habitation such as a car or an abandoned building. Some live in tent communities with other homeless people. Others sleep in alleys or doorways or even in the backyards of empty houses.

Homeless youth who are on their own are more likely to be unsheltered than those who are with family. According to HUD, about 60 percent of unaccompanied youth are without shelter. The high number is at least partly a result of lack of accommodations for youth in homeless shelters. In the entire United States, only four thousand shelter beds are available for unaccompanied youths under age eighteen. This means the majority of unaccompanied homeless youth are forced to struggle for survival on the streets.

Unsheltered homeless youth may seek refuge during the day inside a public library, bus station, or shopping mall, and they may sleep in a park, doorway, or subway tunnel at night. Some couch surf for a night or two with relatives or friends before moving on. Other homeless youth must find whatever shelter they can from the elements or the dangers of the streets. For example, one homeless teen named Mary ran away from an abusive home and slept in a park in Tempe, Arizona. What she referred to as "a cozy little home"[18] was actually the inside of a storm overflow drainage pipe in a local park; she had to squeeze in through the square hole in the concrete lid of the storm drain.

Finding Shelter

Putting a roof over one's head is important for survival. Just being indoors is better than being on the streets or sleeping in a storm drain. But in some cases, homeless youth seek shelter in a building that is unsafe or unhealthy in various ways. This was the case

Some youth shelters, like this one in Oregon, provide a place for young people to pick up a quick snack or a bar of soap. Other shelters offer space for short-term and long-term overnight stays.

for Florida teen Maria Fabian, who was homeless and on her own while in high school. Her mother died when she was six, and she lived with an aunt and uncle until one day they packed up and left, abandoning her. She was completely on her own at age sixteen. Fabian managed to find shelter, living illegally in an abandoned apartment with no heat, running water, or electricity. As she recalls, "At night I would go to bed on a dingy mattress without a box spring. I spent more time staring at the ceiling wondering what was going to happen next than sleeping. Some nights were cold. Some were hot. All of them were scary."[19]

In an emergency situation, homeless youth can seek temporary refuge in a safe house. But there are even fewer beds available nationwide in safe houses than there are in youth shelters, and kids can only stay there for a limited amount of time. The Lutheran Social Service of Minnesota, for example, runs an emergency shelter for youth aged sixteen to twenty. The safe house has only six beds, however, and it only houses kids overnight, from 7:00 p.m. to 9:00 a.m., and not during the day. Still, safe houses like this one provide homeless youth with an option that is better than sleeping on the streets.

The best option long term is a homeless shelter, but even this solution has its obstacles. Most homeless shelters do not accept unaccompanied youth. And even homeless families may have a hard time finding space in a long-term shelter. Many shelters have waiting lists, especially in large cities, and people may have to wait months or even years to get in.

Life in a Homeless Shelter

For those who are able to find space in a homeless shelter, day-to-day life for kids can be a real challenge. For starters, just being in a shelter does not guarantee that families will be able to re-main intact. Large families may not be able to find space together, and many are forced to split up in separate shelters. Parents may spend their days working, job hunting, or searching for a place to live that they can afford. Consequently, many kids in shelters may only see their parents for an hour or two a day.

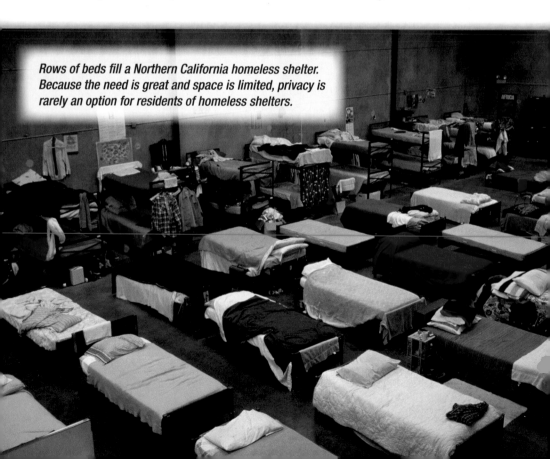

Rows of beds fill a Northern California homeless shelter. Because the need is great and space is limited, privacy is rarely an option for residents of homeless shelters.

Not all shelters are the same; some are large and house hundreds of people, whereas others have room for only a couple dozen people. Some families live in a motel or an apartment-like setting, with one or two rooms, a kitchen or kitchenette, and a private bathroom. But the vast majority of families in shelters must live together in a single room with no cooking facilities, no bathroom, and very little privacy. Homeless teen Kevin Liu lived in a tiny room together with his parents and younger brother; they had to walk down a hallway to use a communal bathroom. Another homeless youth, Dasani, lived crammed together with her family of ten in a single room that measured 520 square feet (48 sq m)—about the size of a large living room. In Dasani's shelter the bathrooms had toilet stalls, like public restrooms, and there was only one bathroom per floor. If the bathroom on one floor was out of order, people had to use a bathroom on a different floor. Dasani's family kept a mop bucket in their room to use as a toilet when the communal bathroom was full or out of order. In most shelters, people have learned not to expect any privacy in the bathrooms—bathtubs may not have partitions around them, showers may lack curtains, and other residents may intrude at any time.

Sleeping arrangements in shelters also vary. Some shelters feature bunk beds, others merely mattresses on the floor. Some kids in shelters sleep on a hard, uncomfortable cot, and others sleep doubled up with another family member in a bed or on a mattress on the floor.

In addition to cramped quarters, a lack of privacy, and barriers to getting a good night's sleep, residents in homeless shelters must also contend with an array of rules and regulations. While many of the rules seem overbearing, they are often intended to provide security. At many shelters, movement in and out of the building by residents is restricted. One homeless teen recalls, "You had to sign out to leave and you were limited on how often you could leave."[20] Most long-term shelters do not have a restriction

> "You had to sign out to leave [the shelter] and you were limited on how often you could leave."[20]
>
> —Homeless teen William.

on how long residents can live there, although the average family stays about nine months. However, shelters do have rules in place that discourage people from staying there too long; for example, residents are not allowed to decorate the walls, have their own furniture in the rooms, or bring in canned goods or microwaves.

Many shelters have strict rules when it comes to security. For example, the Auburn Family Residence, a homeless shelter in New York City, features a tall iron fence and metal detectors. The front door is heavily guarded, and residents' bags are searched for contraband items such as irons and hair dryers, which are considered fire hazards. Locked gates prevent children from playing on the front lawn, which is untended and overgrown with weeds. Visitors are not allowed beyond the front lobby, and children are not allowed to ride the elevators without an adult.

Despite security measures such as these, residents of homeless shelters can find themselves the victims of crime. Though they may not have many possessions, what little they do have must be watched carefully in the shelters. The members of one family were devastated to return to their room and discover all their food stamps had been stolen. Says one homeless teen, "I don't like the shelter. Things get stolen easily."[21]

A State of Disrepair

Although being homeless is never easy, some homeless shelters are relatively clean and pleasant places. This was the case for Reahmaria McMillan, a homeless single mother in Detroit. McMillan recalls, "In 2010 I moved with my girls, then ages 2, 5 and 6, to a shelter. It was clean, with sectioned little rooms set up in a church basement. The workers cooked meals for us and greeted my kids with open arms."[22] For the majority of homeless people, however, life in a shelter is not this comfortable. Many homeless shelters are housed in run-down buildings that are in various states of disrepair. This can profoundly affect life for people inside. Conditions inside shelters range from mildly uncomfortable to downright hazardous. Most shelters are noisy and chaotic, both during the day and at night. Many lack adequate ventilation, working furnaces, and air conditioning, so residents are exposed to stale air and temperature extremes.

LGBTQ Youth in Shelters

About 40 percent of homeless youth identify as lesbian, gay, bisexual, transgender, or questioning (LGBTQ). These young people often face bullying and violence in homeless shelters. According to the NCH, there is a prevalent culture of homophobia in shelters, and there are currently no protections for homeless LGBTQ youth at shelters or other housing services. One homeless young man stated, "Almost all LGBTQ people going into shelters have a fear of them, because it isn't a matter of if it's dangerous, but just how dangerous it will be. It is horrible to live in that fear everyday."

Transgender people are especially at risk of discrimination and bullying. One transgender man who was homeless as a teen stayed in a San Francisco shelter. On his first night there, he awoke to find people screaming at him and throwing water on him. He was so frightened that he fled the shelter in the middle of the night. Some gay shelter residents have had condoms full of urine tossed onto their beds. One found a note on his bed that said, "I hate faggots." Other homeless LGBTQ youth experience violence and assault in the shelters. It is not always the other residents who perpetrate these acts; one bisexual teen girl was assaulted by a janitor in her room at a homeless shelter.

Quoted in Alex Abramovich, "Homeless LGBT Youth Face Discrimination, Violence in Shelter System," Healthy Debate, January 28, 2015. http://healthydebate.ca.

Quoted in Emily Green, "Groundbreaking Shelter for LGBT Homeless Opening in the Mission," *San Francisco Chronicle*, June 16, 2015. http://www.sfchronicle.com.

Some shelters are in old buildings that are badly in need of repair or renovation. Walls may be rotting, covered with mold, and filled with holes. Vermin such as mice and roaches roam freely in many shelters. Sinks in disrepair with leaky faucets can force residents to listen to water dripping night and day. In some shelters, the mattresses are old, torn, and dirty and may be infested with bedbugs or body lice. Some shelters have been cited by the city or state for health code violations, including inoperable smoke alarms, spoiled food, vermin, asbestos, lead paint, inadequate heat, and broken elevators.

Many homeless shelters also lack cleanliness. The communal toilets in some shelters may be clogged by feces or vomit. The communal showers are often moldy and unclean. In some shelters, kids are exposed to drug paraphernalia such as crack pipes left lying on the bathroom floor; vulgarities and other graffiti may be scrawled on the bathroom walls. At Auburn, residents are not allowed to have bleach, so they must sneak it into the shelter or steal it from the janitors if they want to clean the filthy showers and bathroom floors.

Finding Food

Whether living on the streets or in a shelter, getting enough to eat often presents its own set of challenges. Most homeless people do not have a lot of money to buy food or a way to store or cook it. Some homeless people steal, beg, or rummage through trash

When the school semester ends, homeless young people who depend on free and discounted school meals often turn to shelters for food. Shelter food (pictured) is not always the most appetizing or nutritious.

cans for food. Even finding fresh, clean water to drink can be a problem. For example, one man who was homeless as a youth recalls that he and his mother had to get drinking water from a jug they filled in gas station restrooms.

Many shelters and soup kitchens that serve homeless youth provide meals, but these may be difficult for kids to get to—they may have to ride a bus a long way or walk a long distance to reach such places. And some kids prefer to avoid visiting such places for various reasons, such as fear of being returned by the authorities to an abusive home or foster care. Public schools also provide free and reduced-cost breakfast and lunch to low-income and homeless children, but many homeless kids do not go to school.

"I haven't eaten in three days."[24]

—Homeless teen McKenna Costianes.

Most of those who live in homeless shelters have one or more meals provided to them. But the food there is not always very appetizing. Kevin Liu, who lived in a homeless shelter with his family for three years, complained that the food served at the shelter was "disgusting."[23] Often the food in shelters is pre-packaged, and residents must contend with lukewarm or room-temperature food; other times they must wait in line to microwave a frozen meal. Dasani and her siblings often had to wait in line in the shelter's cafeteria for an hour or more before they were able to eat, which they had to do sitting on the cracked linoleum floor of their room. And one night Dasani's shelter served only cold cereal for dinner.

For kids who are homeless on their own, finding food to eat can be an especially harrowing experience. McKenna Costianes, a homeless teen who lives on the streets, says she faces a constant battle to find food. "I haven't eaten in three days,"[24] she says. Homeless people may have to walk long distances to find something to eat, and they often find themselves at the mercy of the elements. In the summertime when temperatures soar, for example, conditions can be brutal, especially in the Southwest. Randy Christensen says, "The idea of the homeless kids being

Roughing It

Child advocate Kevin Ryan, president of Covenant House International, wanted to better understand what unsheltered homeless youth go through. So he decided to spend one night outside in a cardboard box. He recalls:

> After spending a night in a cardboard box as part of Covenant House's Solidarity Sleep Out for homeless youth, I understood much more about the toll "sleeping rough" takes on the hearts and the heads of young people. The cold, the noise, the wind, the fear—I don't know how kids bear it. They become exhausted and, eventually, sick from the cold and the worries that keep them awake. Imagine trying to get a good night's sleep in a subway car, in a rat-infested park, or in a room with someone who trades a bed for the use of your body. Imagine waking up having to figure out the next semiacceptable place to stay!

Kevin Ryan and Tina Kelley, *Almost Home: Helping Kids Move from Homelessness to Hope*. Hoboken, NJ: Wiley, 2012, p. 40.

out in such heat waves, forced to walk blocks or even miles for food or shelter, frightened me."[25]

One homeless teen who moved into a motel room with five other homeless people explained there was no stove, microwave, or refrigerator in the room and no way to cook. Because there was no grocery store nearby, and nowhere to cook, she and her friends got most of their meals from a neighborhood convenience store. They rarely ate fresh fruit or vegetables. She describes a typical meal: "Doritos, you know. Subway if we have money. We buy those top ramens and eat them out of the bag."[26]

Homeless teen Maria Fabian managed to get money for food by selling her old video games. She sold one or two games each day until eventually all the games were gone. "I remember the hunger," Fabian says of this time. "The apartment was cold because there was no heat. It was dark because there was no power. But all I could think about was how hungry I was. All I heard in my system was 'hungry . . . hungry . . . hungry . . . I need to eat.' I didn't have any money."[27]

For teens who are homeless, whether on their own or with a family member, the indignities, discomforts, and hunger can be a real nightmare. For many of these kids, daily life is fraught with peril; they must worry constantly about finding enough to eat and putting a roof over their head in order to survive. At a time in their lives when they should be protected and carefree, these kids are forced to struggle for the basic necessities that most people take for granted.

Chapter 3

Staying Safe and Healthy

Homeless youth face many obstacles that can make stay-ing safe and healthy difficult. Whether they are homeless with their family or on their own, they are more likely to be the victim of violence, physical abuse, and sexual abuse. Homeless kids often live in an environment that makes them more likely to become ill than kids who live in a stable, permanent home—and they can face a variety of stumbling blocks to obtaining health care. In addition, the stress of being homeless leads some kids to take risks with their health, such as experimenting with drugs or alcohol.

Young Victims

The majority of homeless youth live in homeless shelters with one or more family member. But these shelters are not always a safe place to live. They can present hazards and even outright dan-gers for residents. This is especially true for kids, who are more vulnerable and may be less able to take care of or protect them-selves than adults.

Violence is not uncommon in many homeless shelters, par-ticularly those located in high-crime areas. Most shelters are very crowded, and some who stay there may abuse drugs or alcohol, be mentally ill, or have a history of domestic abuse. Just being in a homeless shelter is stressful on its own. These factors all raise the risk for violence, which is one reason that unaccompanied youth tend to avoid adult shelters. One homeless teen who was on his own in Phoenix, for example, was beaten up in a shelter and decided he was better off sleeping in an abandoned house instead. But the potential for becoming the victim of violence exists even for kids who are in a shelter with family members. At many shelters, violent arguments and even knife fights can break out between residents.

The potential for sexual abuse is also high in homeless shelters, even for homeless kids who are with their family. In homeless shelters in the Phoenix area, for example, one in four adult males are registered sex offenders. "Bad things happen there at night,"[28] says Juan, a homeless teen in Phoenix. Indeed, both boys and girls are at risk of being molested or raped in homeless shelters. One twelve-year-old boy complained that a female resident showed pornography to the children and touched his genitals. And a twelve-year-old girl refused to use the shelter's bathroom without a parent along because a man exposed his genitals to her. "I am still scared that someone will come in,"[29] she says. But it is not just other residents who pose a potential threat: Staff members can also be guilty of sexual misconduct. At one shelter, a fourteen-year-old girl was sexually assaulted by a security guard.

> "Kids with no place to stay often come to the attention of pimps, who troll the streets around youth homeless shelters."[30]
>
> —Kevin Ryan, president and CEO of Covenant House.

For some homeless youth, the threat of sexual abuse can spiral into a long-term problem. This is because being homeless puts kids at a higher risk of sex trafficking, especially for kids who are homeless on their own. The Federal Bureau of Investigation estimates that 293,000 homeless youth across the nation are at risk of becoming victims of sexual exploitation such as trafficking and prostitution. Kevin Ryan, president and CEO of Covenant House, explains how traffickers look for homeless kids to exploit:

Kids with no place to stay often come to the attention of pimps, who troll the streets around youth homeless shelters, hang out in pizza parlors and schools, patrol bus terminals and airports, and even send young recruiters to live inside shelters to lure young people into the sex trade. They quickly find the kids who have no strong father figures in their lives, a history of foster care or sexual abuse, broken family bonds, or problems with addiction.[30]

Health Hazards

Whether they are sheltered or unsheltered, homeless youth face a variety of other challenges to their well-being. Keeping themselves and their clothing clean can be difficult without access to showers or laundry facilities. One teen who was homeless on the streets said she had resorted to "bathing" by sneaking into a backyard swimming pool. But even kids who live in shelters may not always be able to bathe regularly if the communal bathrooms are full or out of order. And doing laundry can present similar problems— homeless kids or families may not have access to a laundry room, or they may not have enough money to use the machines. Such difficulties in staying clean and hygienic can contribute to homeless kids falling ill.

Other threats to their health can come from the environment in which they live. Those on the streets are exposed to the weather and the elements, which can sap their energy and ability to fight off illness or infection. Homeless kids who seek refuge in an abandoned building—or even a homeless shelter—may have to contend with mold, which can lead to coughs, sinus infections, and breathing difficulties. Mold can also trigger asthma attacks, as can the presence of roach droppings. Many buildings and shelters have poor indoor air quality due to factors such as dust and grime, inadequate ventilation, and even the presence of animal or human wastes. These things can further compromise the immune system of homeless people. According to the NCFH, homeless kids have twice as

"I have a rat that's 18 inches long. He comes out of the walls and goes in my garbage bag every night."[31]

—A mother who lives in a New York City homeless shelter with her two young children.

Young people without a home or family may turn to prostitution to support themselves. They are also at higher risk of being caught up in sex trafficking schemes.

many ear infections and four times as many respiratory infections as kids who are not homeless.

Buildings and shelters can be home to a variety of vermin such as mice, roaches, and spiders. One woman who lives in a New York City homeless shelter with her two young children says, "I have a rat that's 18 inches long. He comes out of the walls and goes in my garbage bag every night."[31] Sometimes the danger is not as obvious as this, however. A homeless teen girl who lived in an abandoned house discovered several sores on her face and stomach. She did not realize that she had been bitten by a spider. The bites got infected, and because her immune system was run down, the infection spread through her body and required treatment with antibiotics.

Serious Illness and Death

Hunger, poor diet, and malnutrition also contribute to homeless youth being more likely to get sick and stay sick. When the body is run down and lacking in essential nutrients, colds take longer to go away and more easily turn into more serious conditions such as bronchitis or pneumonia. Prolonged hunger and inadequate nutrition can have serious long-term effects such as poor bone and muscle development—a particular problem for growing youth.

Living in unhygienic conditions and crowded shelters also places homeless youth at risk of contracting potentially life-threatening illnesses and diseases. In addition, many homeless kids are not up-to-date on their immunizations, which increases the risk for such diseases. Homeless people are at higher risk of contracting serious communicable diseases such as HIV, hepatitis C, and tuberculosis (TB). In fact, TB, which is spread from one person to another through the air, is becoming epidemic among

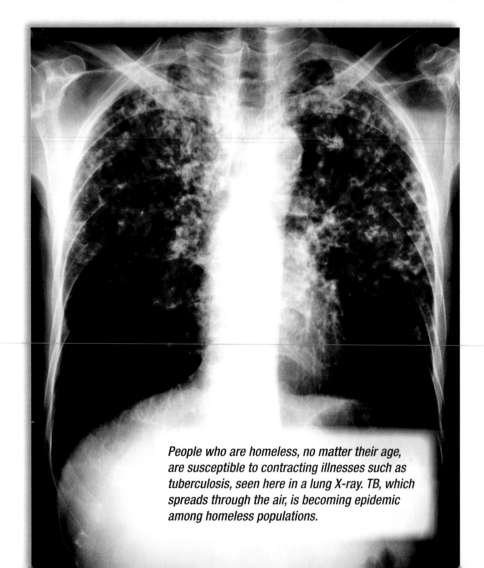

People who are homeless, no matter their age, are susceptible to contracting illnesses such as tuberculosis, seen here in a lung X-ray. TB, which spreads through the air, is becoming epidemic among homeless populations.

homeless populations. It has been identified as a problem in large shelters such as Peachtree-Pines in Atlanta, Georgia, which is the largest homeless shelter in the Southeast. "The homeless are prime candidates for tuberculosis because they typically have greater exposure to cold weather, are in crowded conditions when they stay in shelters, and lack proper nutrition and medical care,"[32] explains a reporter for the *Atlanta Journal-Constitution*. Without proper medical care, which many homeless people lack, TB can be fatal.

In addition to untreated illness, homeless kids face the potential for death from other causes as well. This is particularly true for kids who live on the streets, who can face death from violence, accidents, or exposure to the elements. For example, some homeless people sleep in drainage ditches, a practice that can become deadly in areas such as the Southwest, which is prone to sudden downpours of rain. "Homeless people have drowned after falling asleep in the washes and getting caught in a flash flood,"[33] says Randy Christensen. And in 2010 eight homeless youth in their teens and early twenties who sought shelter in an abandoned New Orleans warehouse and burned trash in a barrel to keep warm died in their sleep when the wood-framed structure caught fire.

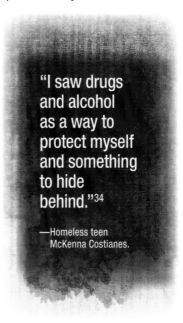

"I saw drugs and alcohol as a way to protect myself and something to hide behind."[34]

—Homeless teen McKenna Costianes.

Substance Abuse

Some homeless youth further endanger their health and well-being by turning to alcohol and/or drugs to deal with the stress of their situation. According to the nonprofit organization DoSomething.org, about 80 percent of homeless youth use drugs or alcohol as a means to deal with the trauma of being homeless. One example is homeless teen McKenna Costianes, who started doing meth to help cope with her depression. "I saw drugs and alcohol as a way to protect myself and something to hide behind,"[34] she says.

Drug and alcohol abuse is more likely among kids who are on their own or on the streets, as opposed to those who are sheltered with family members. But even youth who are in shelters are vulnerable to the lure of a quick fix for the stress and anxiety of being homeless. One homeless teen, Wayne, explains what happened after he moved into a shelter with his mom:

When my mom and I first got to the shelter, I was pretty scared. I was fourteen and kind of scrawny for my age, and there were a lot of older kids there who were bigger than me. I had to walk past these older kids and men outside when I came back from school, and they all looked tough, like, street. But at least we had a roof over our heads. Things would turn out OK. Or so I thought. But then my mom found a job and was gone all the time, and I was alone in the shelter every day after school, sometimes it was ten or eleven at night when she got home. There were these guys who hung out in the bathroom smoking pot, and so I decided to try it one day. And . . . instant relief. Everything got mellow and my problems just melted away, like, floated off on a cloud. I thought I would try it just once, but once I did, then I couldn't wait to feel like that again.[35]

Although these substances may provide temporary relief, in the long run they only wind up making the problem worse. Indeed, drug and alcohol abuse can make kids more vulnerable to being assaulted or physically abused. In the long term, it can lead to health problems, including heart abnormalities and cirrhosis (or scarring) of the liver, an irreversible condition. Kids who abuse drugs and alcohol also place themselves at risk of dying from a drug overdose or alcohol poisoning. And for kids who are homeless, medical attention for such emergencies may not be a viable or timely option.

Finding Health Care

Finding health care, whether for a medical emergency or for routine problems, can be difficult for homeless people. There are

Sharing Space with Cockroaches

Pediatrician Randy Christensen works with homeless teens in the Phoenix, Arizona, area. In his years of working with this population, he has seen many disturbing things, some of which clearly threaten health and safety. "I can't tell you the number of cockroaches I've taken out of ears," says Christensen. In one instance, a teen girl who was screaming in pain and holding her hand over one ear sought his help. The girl was living in an empty dumpster, as Christensen explains:

> The kids would lie down to sleep in abandoned houses and filthy camps, and the cockroaches would run right inside their ears. Baby cockroaches in particular. Every few moments the pain lessened, and she sighed with relief. Then a moment later the screaming began again. The pain came when the insect pinched its spiny claws into her tender eardrum. When it relaxed its hold, the pain diminished. . . . I led the girl into an exam room and examined her ear. Sure enough, there was a large bug deep in her ear. Not only was it a huge cockroach, but it had also wiggled way up the ear canal.

Quoted in Lisette Hilton, "Mobile Clinic to the Rescue," *Contemporary Pediatrics*, April 1, 2015. http://contemporarypediatrics.modernmedicine.com.

Randy Christensen and Rene Denfeld, *Ask Me Why I Hurt: The Kids Nobody Wants and the Doctor Who Heals Them.* New York: Broadway, 2011, p. 70.

health clinics that serve low-income and homeless populations, but many such clinics are underfunded and understaffed. In addition, parents may not have a way to get their kids to a clinic if it is far away. And many street kids are leery of seeking help from clinics and other social services because they do not want to come to the attention of authorities.

As a result of these factors, many homeless kids do not see a doctor regularly—some not even when they are sick. This can lead to worsening health problems, such as an ongoing cough that develops into something more serious. Asthma in particular is often left untreated, in part because of a lack of access to health care or money to pay for the necessary medication. Some kids with asthma may need to use a nebulizer—a device that vaporizes the asthma medication to make it easier to inhale and therefore more effective. But even if they can get a nebulizer—for example, from a free clinic—they may not have a place to plug it in.

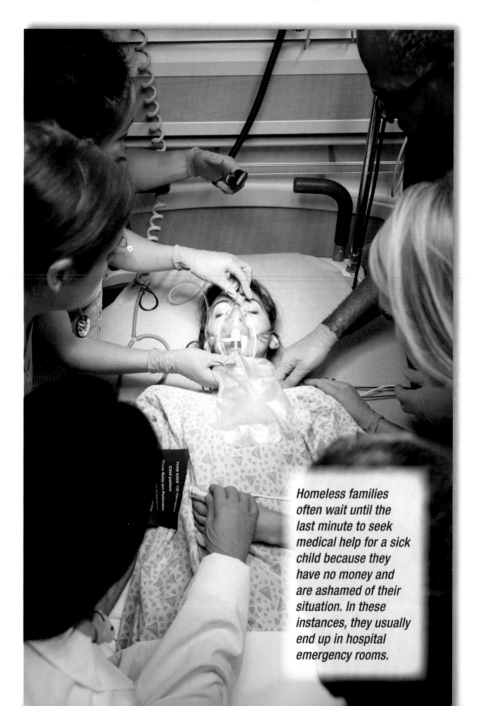

Homeless families often wait until the last minute to seek medical help for a sick child because they have no money and are ashamed of their situation. In these instances, they usually end up in hospital emergency rooms.

Trafficking of Homeless Youth

Prostitution is a common problem in the teen homeless population. Desperate for money and sometimes for attention from an adult, some kids turn to prostitution. Others are coerced or forced to sell themselves. Either way, it rarely works out well for the teen. Some wind up pregnant or with a sexually transmitted disease, others may be beaten or even killed, and all suffer from a devastating blow to their self-esteem.

This problem is not limited to one state or one city. But one study, done in 2015, provides a glimpse into the world of teen homelessness and prostitution. The study was conducted in New Orleans, Louisiana, by Covenant House and Loyola University. The study found that nearly 25 percent of homeless youth arriving at the Covenant House shelter had been forced into prostitution. "The numbers tell a sad and horrific story," says Covenant House New Orleans executive director Jim Kelly. "These are good kids who have experienced years of abuse, violence and trauma."

Quoted in Covenant House, "New Study Shows 25 Percent of Homeless Youth Victims of Trafficking or Sexual Labor Before Finding Shelter at Covenant House," March 9, 2015. www.covenanthouse.org.

Because of a lack of access to health care or insurance, many homeless people only seek medical attention when their condition becomes intolerable. Often their only option is a trip to the emergency room. Pediatrician Randy Christensen says that because of the difficulties involved in getting to a doctor or clinic, when kids get sick, they often receive medical treatment "very, very late." This can result in small problems becoming much bigger problems that are more difficult to treat. For example, "The ear infection—it's not just a little red," says Christensen. "You look at it, and there's pus coming out of it."[36]

For homeless youth who lack insurance, the consequences can be especially grueling. One homeless teen was diagnosed with rheumatoid arthritis, an extremely painful and often debilitating condition that affects the joints. But she was unable to seek treatment, as she explains: "Once I was on the streets I lost my MaineCare health insurance so I couldn't go to the doctors or get medication for my condition. I went without meds for a year and the pain was terrible."[37]

Indeed, many homeless kids do not have health insurance at all. This is especially true for homeless kids who are on their own. A major obstacle for these kids is the fact that most of them do not have identification. Most runaways, for example, do not have a driver's license or access to their birth certificate. This lack of identification can limit access to services, including insurance and health care. Even visiting a dentist can be difficult, leading to issues such as untreated cavities and tooth abscesses.

Millions of young people find themselves locked in a struggle to stay safe and healthy without a permanent home. In some cases, they are falling ill or even dying because they have no place to stay besides a run-down shelter or a rodent-infested abandoned warehouse. Some cannot even get adequate health care because they lack money or insurance. With all these strikes against them, the millions of homeless youth in this country are placed at a great disadvantage in life.

Chapter 4

Getting an Education

For youth who are homeless, going to school and getting an education can be a daunting task. This is especially true for those who are homeless on their own, but even kids who are homeless with family members face many obstacles when it comes to school success. Being homeless puts these kids at risk of falling behind, failing a grade, and dropping out. Tamara Haag, who oversees the homeless education program in Clarke County, Georgia, sees firsthand the effects of homelessness on young people. "They have additional barriers to academic success that other students might not," she says. "The likelihood they are able to succeed and graduate is lessened by being homeless."[38]

Moving a Lot

Most homeless families move frequently, which means that homeless kids change schools a lot—sometimes with little or no warning. As a result of moving so often, homeless kids miss a lot of school. They may also have to change schools each time they move. According to the NCFH, in a given year, 97 percent of homeless children move, some as many as three times; 40 percent attend two different schools in a year, and 28 percent attend three or more different schools in a year. Under federal law, public schools must ensure that homeless students have access to a free education; the law also grants homeless students the right to remain in the same school even if their family moves to a different district. In practice, however, this does not always happen; consequently, many homeless kids switch schools each time they move. For example, Dasani, a homeless girl in New York City, once had to switch schools three times in six weeks.

43

Poor attendance or having to change schools often can leave homeless kids behind the rest of the class. Consequently, they may feel disconnected and lost during lessons or when trying to do homework. Having to move suddenly, without warning, can be traumatic and jarring to kids and can add to the confusion they feel at school. According to Kevin Ryan of Covenant House, each time a kid changes schools, it can set them back academically four to six months. One nine-year-old girl, Yoselin, moved with her family from one homeless shelter to another. By the time her family finally moved in to a shelter that had a school close enough for Yoselin to attend, she had missed more than a month of school. "I think I'm a little behind,"[39] Yoselin confessed.

As a result of frequent moves and switching schools often, homeless kids may also see their grades suffer. This happened to fifteen-year-old Aliah, who had to switch schools nine times during her first year of high school. She says the instability of being homeless had a big effect on her education. "I was failing all the time," she recalls. "How do you expect to keep up your grades going to nine schools during your freshman year?"[40]

> "I was failing all the time. How do you expect to keep up your grades going to nine schools during your freshman year?"[40]
>
> —Homeless teen Aliah.

Getting to School

Along with moving a lot, lack of transportation poses another obstacle to getting an education. The mere act of getting to school—on time or at all—can be difficult for homeless youth. Kids who live far from their school—whether in a shelter, a relative's house, or somewhere else—often struggle to get to school. Their family may not have a car, or a parent may need to use the car to get to work, leaving the kids to find their own way to school. In some cases buses, either school buses or city buses, are available, but they may require long rides with many bus changes, and the kids may have to walk a long way to get to a bus stop. The trip to school

Getting to school can be difficult for homeless youth. If a parent or older sibling cannot accompany a young child on the subway, for instance, the child might be forced to stay home from school.

can be a lengthy ordeal for homeless kids; in some big cities, for example, the bus ride to school can take a couple of hours.

In other cases, despite a federal law mandating that schools provide transportation for homeless kids regardless of how far they live from the school, no buses are available. In some urban areas, the subway is the only option, but some kids are too young to ride the subway alone. So they may end up missing the school day altogether if a parent or older sibling is sick or has an appointment and cannot accompany them. In New York City, for example, when homeless shelters became too full in 2015, the city placed about 750 families in hotels in far-flung regions of the city. Many of these families were placed in hotels that were a long distance from their children's schools. This resulted in dozens of children, accompanied by their parents, being transported to school via bus, ferry, and subway starting at 5:30 a.m. One such youth, a high school girl, had to make a two-hour commute each way on two subway trains, a ferry, and a city bus. Yet this grueling commute was her only option if she wanted to get to school

Barriers to School Success

According to James P. Canfield, a licensed clinical social worker and author of *School-Based Practice with Children and Youth Experiencing Homelessness*, homeless kids face a number of obstacles that can impede their success in school. He explains:

> Bus stops can be a major barrier. Or more so, the embarrassment of other students knowing a stop is for kids at a shelter can make life very difficult for homeless children and youth. . . . Moving a bus stop one block away so that the kids staying in a shelter could be dropped off at a recreation center and park rather than in front of a shelter anecdotally reduced bullying and problems amongst the students. . . . Some homeless children do not wish to seek services for fear of being "outed," meaning their peers will find out about their situation. The small act of having the same sweatshirt as other people could go a long way to helping the child feel welcomed and a part of the school.

James P. Canfield, *School-Based Practice with Children and Youth Experiencing Homelessness*. New York: Oxford University Press, 2015, p. 107.

on time. And, as she explains, "At my school, I can only have so many times to be late."[41]

As a result of such difficulties, by the time some of these kids finally get to school they are exhausted. They may arrive late and miss out on lessons and important instructions. Some days they may not even be able to get to school at all. And being frequently tired, tardy, or absent can make it harder for them to keep up in class.

Hard to Focus

Even homeless kids who do not move or change schools a lot can have other distractions that make learning difficult. It may be hard for them to focus at school and hard to do homework in the shelter. "There's a lot of chaos in homeless students' personal life,"[42] Tamara Haag explains. This chaos can present significant obstacles to the success of homeless kids in school.

Concentrating on schoolwork can be difficult for homeless kids, who may be tired, hungry, and stressed. Students who sleep in shelters may have trouble sleeping due to noise, discomfort, and anxiety. One eight-year-old homeless boy, Lucho, has a hard time staying awake in school because he does not sleep well at night. His bed at the shelter is very hard, and he is constantly worried about having to move to a new shelter. A lack of sleep and high levels of anxiety can take their toll on kids. High school English teacher Sonya Shpilyuk explains that many of her homeless students "have this defeated look on their faces. . . . They're tired, and they're hungry, and it's stressful because they don't know where they're going after school."[43]

Doing homework can be another challenge for homeless students. They may experience the same difficulties concentrating on homework as they do on class work. In addition, homeless kids may have limited access to computers and the Internet—or none at all. Many homeless kids rely on the public library for a quiet place to study and for computers and a connection to the Internet. But in many communities, the number of computers available and the hours the library is open have been reduced due to budget cuts. Some try to do their homework in the shelter, but that is not usually a good option. Rooms in some shelters do not have a desk or chair, so kids may have to do their homework sitting on a mattress or the bare floor. In addition to not having a good place to do their homework, they may not have the supplies they need to complete an assignment, such as paper, colored pencils, and glue. And one

> "[Homeless students] have this defeated look on their faces. . . . They're tired, and they're hungry, and it's stressful because they don't know where they're going after school."[43]
>
> —High school English teacher Sonya Shpilyuk.

homeless girl who lived without electricity had trouble doing her homework at night because it was hard to read in the dark. Additionally, many homeless kids whose parents are at work or otherwise absent may have no one to turn to for help with homework.

These difficulties focusing in school and getting homework done can contribute to homeless youth doing poorly in school. Says William, who was homeless as a youth, "My grades went kaputz when my mother and I lived in the shelters."[44] Homeless students also tend to score lower on standardized tests. According to the NCFH, only 11.4 percent of homeless high school students were proficient in math, and only 14.6 percent were proficient in reading—both well below national averages. Poor grades can put homeless students at risk of being held back a grade. According to the DOE, half of homeless children nationwide are held back one grade, and more than 20 percent are held back for multiple grades.

Self-Consciousness

Another factor that can compromise a homeless student's success in school is the stigma associated with being homeless. Aliah, who was homeless throughout most of her childhood, felt this stigma sharply at each new school she attended. "No one really talked to me, and I felt like all I had was my mama to talk to," she says. "I would text my mama nonstop, which is even more embarrassing when someone asks, 'Who are you texting?'"[45]

Like Aliah, many homeless kids feel isolated at school and have difficulties feeling like they fit in. Some homeless kids may have a hard time keeping themselves and their clothes clean, which can make them stick out at school and suffer teasing from their classmates. Some may even have to sneak into the school bathroom in the mornings to wash up and brush their teeth, hoping that other students do not see them and figure out they are homeless.

In addition, most homeless kids do not have a lot of clothes, which can affect their self-esteem. Maria Fabian, who was homeless for a year while in high school, was terribly self-conscious about the fact that she only had two shirts. She explains how she coped with this: "I always wore a jacket to school. If I zipped up the jacket, no one could see that I was wearing the same shirt every other day."[46] The clothes homeless kids do have may be old and worn or not in style. And although most homeless kids appreciate receiving donated clothing, "once in a while they'd like to wear something without some other kid's name written in it,"[47] explains newspaper columnist Ann Brenoff. Their dignity may suffer a further blow due to teasing over what they are wearing. One homeless girl who wore a donated pink sweatsuit suffered ridicule when the other kids teased her about wearing her pajamas to school. Such teasing is especially difficult for children and teens to

Donated clothes might be the only clothing available to homeless young people. Even those who appreciate these donated items sometimes long for new and more stylish clothing.

Teased in Middle School

Dawn Loggins, a homeless high school student who was abandoned by her drug-abusing parents, knows firsthand how the struggle to keep clean can have a devastating effect on a homeless kid. She and her brother stayed in a decrepit house that lacked electricity and running water. They would sometimes shower in the restroom of a local park after the park was empty. Other times they would fill water jugs from the spigots in the park bathroom and haul them back to the house to use for cooking or to flush the toilet. When Dawn was in middle school, she and her brother lived with their grandmother for a while—but conditions there were not much better. "She never really explained to me and my brother the importance of bathing regularly," says Dawn. "And our house was really disgusting. We had cockroaches everywhere. And we had trash piled literally 2 feet high. We'd have to step over it to get anywhere in the house." With no one to help teach her about cleanliness and personal hygiene, Dawn would often go two to three months without showering. And she would wear the same filthy dress to school for weeks at a time. Consequently, she found herself the subject of ridicule by her classmates in middle school. "It was the worst," she recalls. "I would come home crying because the teasing was so bad."

Quoted in Vivian Kuo, "From Scrubbing Floors to Ivy League: Homeless Student to Go to Dream College," CNN, June 8, 2012. www.cnn.com.

bear, because most do not want to stick out or be different from the other kids at school. "They really want to fit in and blend in and look like everyone else,"[48] says Barbara Duffield of the National Association for the Education of Homeless Children and Youth.

All of these factors can compound feelings of self-consciousness and shame over being homeless. When combined with the stress and fatigue that often go along with being homeless, these feelings can make it harder for kids to concentrate and do well in school.

Acting Out

The difficulties of dealing with being homeless can affect kids in school in other ways as well. Sociologist Yvonne M. Vissing describes the psychological impact of homelessness on kids as being worse than the physical impact of having no home. The trauma of being homeless can result in long-term emotional scars and can lead to feelings of anger and resentment. These feelings can be very confusing for kids, and they may not always know how to deal with them successfully or appropriately.

Shame leads some kids to act out rather than ask for help. For example, homeless teen Jonas was too embarrassed to admit to anyone at school, teachers or classmates, that his family had to sleep in a car. He was cold most nights, and he worried about his family's situation. He started talking back to his teachers, not doing his homework, and walking out of class without permission. His behavior at school resulted in him receiving detention both before and after school. Rather than being punishment, detention actually provided him with a safe, warm place to go in the mornings and afternoons and allowed him to avoid his difficult situation a little while longer each day.

According to the National Health Care for the Homeless Council (HCH), kids who are or have ever been homeless are more likely to behave aggressively. They may start to act out in school and become difficult for their teachers to control. For example, twelve-year-old Taylor, who was homeless with his mother, was deeply embarrassed when the other kids at school found out he lived in a shelter and began to tease him. He had problems concentrating because of the stress of being homeless, and his classmates further teased him about his low grades. Taylor felt angry all the time, and he started getting into fights at school.

Like Taylor, many other homeless kids have reacted to the teasing and bullying of their peers by becoming bullies themselves. This was the case with homeless teen Maria Fabian, who explains:

> I discovered that I could talk smack and pick on people too. I figured out that if I break someone first, they'll never break me. I knew it was mean, but it was my way of defending myself. I became a bully. . . . The moment I met

51

someone I picked on her. If there was a new student, I picked on him. I picked on anyone I could just to let everyone know where I stood on the classroom totem pole. I talked hard on anyone who came at me to make sure that everyone around me knew what I felt, especially the teachers.[49]

One day in class, Fabian got into a fight with another girl while the teacher was out of the room. After throwing a punch that knocked the other girl to the floor, Fabian was suspended for ten days. Situations such as these, in which homeless kids act out in school, bully other students, and are given detention or even suspension, can make it tougher for them to get an education.

Homelessness can be deeply frustrating for young people. They may act out their frustrations by getting into fights or engaging in other disruptive behaviors at school.

Dropping Out

The obstacles to getting an education are so high for many homeless youth that, at some point, they begin to lose hope. In such circumstances, according to Ralph da Costa Nunez, president and chief executive of the Institute for Children, Poverty and Homelessness, "What you're going to find is more homeless students dropping out, repeating a grade."[50]

Indeed, according to a 2014 report from Tufts University, homeless youth are 87 percent more likely to stop going to school altogether. This dropout rate is especially alarming in light of the fact that there are nearly 1.4 million homeless students in the nation—more than three hundred thousand of whom are in high school, according to the National Center for Homeless Education. This means that homeless teens are at a high risk of winding up without a high school diploma, which sharply impedes their ability to find a job and earn a living as an adult.

One young man who was homeless as a child recalled that his family moved so often that he dropped out of school in the third grade. For homeless teen Marcy, moving from one shelter to another left her so depleted that she dropped out of high school. She explains:

> After we got evicted, we stayed with my aunt for a while. Then my parents moved us from one friend's house to another. And then we moved into a homeless shelter, but we weren't there long before we had to move again. One year we moved four times. And every time we moved I had to start a new school. In class I never understood what they were talking about. I felt stupid because I couldn't do the homework, couldn't pass the tests. By the time I was in tenth grade I just gave up. I quit going. Looking back, I wish I had stuck it out and graduated. But back then, it was like torture. I just couldn't do it anymore, so I dropped out.[51]

The struggle to keep up in school often means homeless kids wind up with a poor education. For those who find the struggle too hard and give up as Marcy did, their path to getting an education is cut short. With limited education or with no high school diploma, many homeless youth have little hope of bettering their lives.

Chapter 5

Efforts to Help Homeless Youth

In 2015 the US government spent $4.5 billion on various efforts to address homelessness. And there are many programs in communities throughout the United States as well to help homeless youth with the array of issues they face. Some address health care needs, whereas others deal with helping homeless youth find shelter and get an education. In some cases a member of the public steps up to help a homeless child in need. Together, these programs and individual efforts are an important part of the effort to solve the problem of youth homelessness.

Health Clinics

Many communities across the nation have clinics that offer health care and other services to homeless youth. The HCH is a nationwide group that provides support to more than two hundred clinics in all fifty states. HCH clinics provide a wide range of health care, counseling, and referral services to homeless youth of any age.

In addition to stationary clinics, many cities throughout the United States have mobile clinics that provide a range of medical services to homeless people, including homeless youth. The Children's Health Fund, which launched in 1987, has more than fifty mobile clinics in the United States that provide medical care to homeless and low-income kids and their families. This nonprofit organization often partners with other groups that offer mobile health care to kids. These medical vans typically contain exam rooms, a nurse's station, and a registration and waiting area. They also contain a supply of commonly needed medications, and many also stock supplies of blankets, spare clothing, and toiletries such as soap, toothbrushes, and sanitary pads.

Some communities have their own medical clinics specifically for homeless kids. These can be stationary or mobile and typically include vans or RVs that travel to areas where homeless youth tend to gather. They usually offer free basic first aid, referrals, and health advice, as well as services such as crisis intervention, emergency shelter, and counseling. Some mobile medical clinics are operated by a volunteer medical staff, though others have full-time paid medical professionals on staff. One example is the Bridge Mobile Medical Van in the Boston area. Another is the Crews'n Healthmobile, which operates in and around Phoenix. It is run by pediatrician Randy Christensen and a staff of more than thirty health care providers. It includes a freestanding clinic as well as three mobile medical units and provides health care to homeless and at-risk youth. The van interiors look just like a small doctor's office. Each is typically staffed by a doctor, a nurse, a case manager, and sometimes a social worker. Crews'n vans visit areas with high numbers of homeless kids, such as shelters and youth centers, and treat about eighteen hundred homeless kids a year.

One homeless youth helped by the Crews'n Healthmobile is eighteen-year-old Brittany, who had been abusing alcohol. Brittany visited the Crews'n van dozens of times, and the staff helped her stop drinking. Then during one of her routine checkups, the doctor discovered she had type 2 diabetes. This disease is manageable with the right medications and proper medical care, but both of those can be hard to come by for someone in Brittany's situation. "When you're homeless, there's not a whole lot of options out there, but the clinics—and even those have copays,"[52] she says. Fortunately for Brittany and other homeless kids, medical care and medicine at the Crews'n Healthmobile are totally free. But Crews'n medical professionals go above and beyond to help kids, and Brittany gives them credit for helping her return to school and graduate. She says of the Crews'n staff, "You feel like you're home, like there's someone there for you. It's almost like you get a mental hug when you leave."[53]

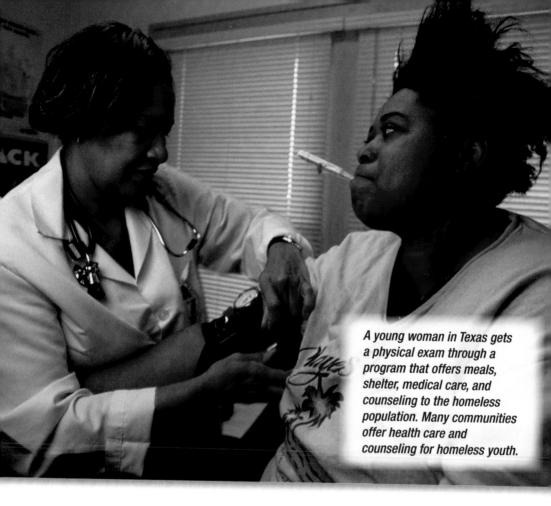

A young woman in Texas gets a physical exam through a program that offers meals, shelter, medical care, and counseling to the homeless population. Many communities offer health care and counseling for homeless youth.

Homeless Youth Outreach

Various organizations offer assistance to homeless youth in the form of food, shelter, job training, and transitional living programs. Many communities have their own programs to help homeless and runaway youth find emergency shelter, counseling, health care, and legal aid. One example is the Homeless Youth Network in Houston, Texas, which coordinates resources for housing and other support services from participating organizations in the Houston area.

There are also many national organizations, such as the United Way, the Salvation Army, the NCH, and the NAEH, that oversee and operate homeless shelters. One of the nation's largest privately funded agencies that works with homeless kids is Covenant House. It has locations in sixteen major US cities in states ranging from Alaska to Florida. Covenant House provides homeless and runaway youth food, shelter, health care, crisis care, drug abuse treatment, legal services, and educational support such as preparing for the GED and applying for college scholarships. It also has outreach vans that drive around dangerous neighborhoods and look for youth who may be in need of help.

Other organizations offer transitional housing, in which homeless youth stay while they learn the skills they need in order to become self-sufficient adults. Transitional housing programs also offer various services such as vocational training. One example is the GATES Transitional Living Program in Tampa, Florida, which serves homeless girls ages sixteen to twenty-one. The GATES facility is a group home that provides each girl a room to live in as well as a common area where they can socialize and watch TV. During their stay—which varies in length but is usually about nine to twelve months—the girls receive life-skills training, counseling and substance abuse services, and assistance in finding a job and an apartment of their own.

Another program that offers transitional housing to homeless youth is the Bridge Over Troubled Waters program in Boston. The Bridge has a team of counselors, teachers, and health care volunteers to help homeless kids put their lives back on track. It offers a transitional day program, in which homeless youth can do laundry, take a shower, eat a hot meal, meet with a case manager, use computers, and learn life skills. The Bridge also offers a transitional living program, which provides housing, counseling and substance abuse services, medical care, help with goal setting, life-skills training, and job-training programs. One homeless teen the Bridge helped is eighteen-year-old Malcolm, who relates, "If I didn't have Bridge, I would be couch surfing or sleeping outside. I like the people at the Bridge Shelter. Everyone knows who I am. . . . I know that step by step I will get up to a good place in this world."[54]

"I like the people at the Bridge Shelter. Everyone knows who I am. . . . I know that step by step I will get up to a good place in this world."[54]

—Homeless teen Malcolm, who found housing at the Bridge Shelter.

57

Help with School and More

Many communities throughout the United States have efforts in place to help homeless youth obtain an education and get their diploma or GED. These efforts include providing transportation, school supplies, monthly stipends, and even referrals for health care services for homeless students. One example is the Clarke County School District Homeless Education Program (HEP) in Athens, Georgia, which provides transportation from shelters to schools, book bags filled with school supplies, and services such as tutoring and counseling to homeless youth. The HEP also provides after-school programs, emergency supplies, and toiletry items to homeless students. Another way the HEP helps homeless students is by allowing them to enroll and attend school even if they do not yet have all the required paperwork, such as immunization records. Lenore Katz, a counselor at one of the district's high schools who coordinates with the HEP, says, "We make sure that all homeless students feel like they have some stability in their lives, so that they can concentrate on what they are in school for, which is go to their classes, do their work, get their credit and get their high school diploma."[55]

Several nonprofit organizations provide educational help to homeless youth as well. For example, Youth on Their Own (YOTO), located in Tucson, Arizona, helps homeless youth ages thirteen to twenty-one graduate high school. YOTO works with almost every school in Tucson, providing support services such as a monthly stipend of $125 for good attendance and good grades, tutoring and mentoring, clothing, help finding health care, and referrals to shelters or other safe places to sleep. YOTO provides assistance for approximately fifteen hundred students per

"We make sure that all homeless students feel like they have some stability in their lives, so that they can concentrate on what they are in school for, which is go to their classes, do their work, get their credit and get their high school diploma."[55]

—Lenore Katz, a high school counselor in Athens, Georgia.

A small group of Covenant House residents in Detroit, Michigan, talk about their achievements since arriving at the shelter. The organization provides food, shelter, health care, legal services, and educational support to homeless youth in sixteen US cities.

year; throughout its thirty-year history it has helped more than fifteen thousand homeless youth stay in school and obtain their diplomas. Monica, a student who was helped by YOTO, says it provided food and stipends, which helped her remain on track to graduate. She praises the program for enabling her to attend college and says, "I intend to create the life I didn't have growing up as a child."[56]

Schools for the Homeless

A few cities have schools devoted expressly to working with homeless kids. One such school is the Monarch School of San Diego, California, which provides an array of services beyond education, including transportation, meals, clothing, showers and laundry facilities, medical care (including vision screenings and glasses), mental health care, and more. Beginning in 1987 as a single classroom and gradually developing into a full K–12 school, Monarch provides almost 450 students per year with a safe place in which to learn. Junior, an eighteen-year-old student at Monarch School, says, "The staff looks after you, and they aren't judging

Birthday Dreams

Homeless children rarely have birthday parties. Birthday Dreams, a group that gives birthday parties to homeless kids in the Puget Sound area in Washington State, is trying to change that. The group's volunteers bake cakes and host birthday parties for the region's homeless children. One homeless mother says, "Birthday Dreams has had a huge impact on our child's life. If it was not for Birthday Dreams, he would not have had a birthday."

Birthday Dreams holds a group party every month at various businesses, nonprofits, and shelters, including YWCAs and the Microsoft store in Bellevue, Washington. The group made it possible for one parent, who was recently laid off, to give his daughter Aleah a birthday party, complete with cake, cotton candy, paper hats, and a brand-new bicycle. As rewarding as it is for children to receive birthday parties and presents, Birthday Dreams co-creator and executive director Chris Spahn says the best gift they get is faith in their parents. "He didn't just give up and let her birthday pass without notice," says Spahn of Aleah's dad. "He showed his daughter that regardless of life's circumstances, the day she was born is a day worth celebrating."

Quoted in Elizabeth Ralston, "Doing Good: Birthday Dreams for All," ParentMap, January 2, 2014. www .parentmap.com.

us for what we've been through. I feel comfortable here and get my work done."[57] A former student adds, "It felt like we were a family. . . . We were able to grow together, bring our grades up, learn to be better students, and find a deeper purpose."[58]

Another school that serves homeless youth is Broome Street Academy (BSA) in Manhattan, New York. The BSA is a public charter high school that, unlike most charter schools, does not charge a fee to attend. The academy gives admissions preference to at-risk students such as homeless youth, youth in foster care, and youth from low-performing schools. Founded in 2011, the BSA provides both academic and nonacademic services to its students through its partner agency, the Door. The Door provides a wide variety of services, such as counseling, food, health care, and legal aid, reproductive health and education, college prep and tutoring, ESOL classes, career counseling, and confidentially provided housing. Sam, who attended the academy, encourages prospective students: "At BSA, you get a clean slate. Your teachers and staff are dedicated to helping you succeed."[59] Enrollment at the academy was 327 students for the 2014–2015 school year.

Individual Efforts

For some homeless youth, it was a personal effort on the part of a caring individual that made the difference. For Maria Fabian, that caring individual was a sympathetic teacher, Miss Jackson. When Fabian confided to her teacher that she was hungry one day, Jackson bought her a sandwich. Over lunch, Fabian told Jackson about being homeless and alone in her dark apartment. Jackson immediately set her up with a social worker, and Fabian was soon living in a transitional housing program that helped her learn the life skills she needed to become independent. Fabian has never forgotten the kindness her teacher showed her that day, and she strives to do the same for others. Today when she sees a homeless person panhandling, Fabian helps out by bringing them something to eat.

Dawn Loggins was in a similar situation after her parents abandoned her during the summer before her senior year in high school. She wanted to continue attending the same school and graduate in the spring, but her choices were limited. If she went to the Department of Social Services, she would likely be placed in a foster home and might have to change schools. In addition, because she would turn eighteen during the

> "[At the Monarch School] it felt like we were a family. . . . We were able to grow together, bring our grades up, learn to be better students, and find a deeper purpose."[58]
>
> —Homeless teen Junior.

spring semester, she would be considered an adult and would no longer qualify for such services. So Loggins was essentially on her own. In her case it was a middle school bus driver and custodian named Sheryl Kolton who stepped up to lend a hand. Kolton knew who Loggins was, but did not know her very well. Nevertheless, when the high school guidance counselor called to ask if Loggins could live with her for a year, Kolton readily agreed.

A Monarch School student reads an eye chart during an exam conducted by a volunteer optometrist. Eye exams are just one of the many services provided at this San Diego, California, school for homeless youth.

True Colors Fund

Singer and songwriter Cyndi Lauper, who was once homeless herself as a teen, decided to fund a thirty-bed homeless shelter for LGBTQ youth. Based in Manhattan, the shelter opened in September 2011. Lauper sought to open this shelter, named True Colors Residence, because up to 40 percent of homeless youth in the United States are LGBTQ, and there are very few shelters specifically for them. Since the shelter's inception, the True Colors Fund has expanded to a nationwide nonprofit that focuses on online networking. For example, the Forty to None Network is an online research and networking community open to advocates, government officials, service providers, and others affected by the issue of LGBTQ homelessness.

Many youth across the United States have been helped in some way by Lauper's True Colors Fund and intend to work to help other LGBTQ people who have been homeless. Cameron Patterson of Seattle, Washington, for example, says she wants to advocate for other LGBTQ youth who are homeless. "My biggest dream is to use my own insights and experiences . . . to change the lives of youth who are experiencing some of the same hardships and discrimination I did."

Quoted in True Colors Fund, "40 of the Forty—2015 List," 2015. https://truecolorsfund.org.

Both Fabian and Loggins were helped by sympathetic staff members at their school. In other cases, though, homeless kids have benefited from the kindness of individuals or entire families. For example, Wayne, who lived in a homeless shelter with his mom while attending high school, found himself suddenly on the streets after she abandoned him, moving away suddenly one day without a word. Since the shelter did not allow unaccompanied youth to stay there, he was sent to a youth shelter instead. Wayne explains what happened next:

> They told me there weren't enough beds at the youth shelter. But I couldn't stay at the adult shelter with my mom

gone. I didn't know what I was going to do—I mean, I was about to be put out on the streets! I remember I was having lunch in the cafeteria that day, and this guy I knew from class noticed I looked down, so he started asking me what was going on. I just told him everything. I told him I had no place else to go. And he looked at me and he said, "You do now."[60]

The family of Wayne's classmate welcomed him into their home, where he lived for a year while in high school. He considers himself very lucky to have been taken in by a caring family; most homeless youth do not have such an opportunity. In large part this may be because there is so little awareness of youth homelessness.

An Intractable Problem

Homelessness among children and teens in the United States poses many problems that are not easy to solve. Many people are not aware of how many youth are homeless in this country or even that they exist at all. It is a problem that cries out for a solution, as the NCFH explains in its report, *America's Youngest Outcasts*:

> If we continue to look away, this problem will grow worse, and the long-term costs to our society will dwarf the costs of making this issue a priority now. We must mobilize a comprehensive response and pay attention to the millions of children in this country who have no home to call their own—or another generation of children will be permanently marginalized and lost.[61]

"We must mobilize a comprehensive response and pay attention to the millions of children in this country who have no home to call their own— or another generation of children will be permanently marginalized and lost."[61]

—The National Center on Family Homelessness.

64

It is often said that children are the future; but for many homeless youth, that future may not be very bright. Many communities and individuals throughout the nation are working to help change that. In the future, such efforts may bring hope to the millions of homeless youth for whom the path to success in life is so uncertain.

Source Notes

Introduction: Kids Living in the Shadows

1. William, "I, Too, Am One of the Estimated 22,000 Homeless Children in New York," *Guardian* (Manchester), January 1, 2014. www.theguardian.com.
2. Randy Christensen and Rene Denfeld, *Ask Me Why I Hurt: The Kids Nobody Wants and the Doctor Who Heals Them*. New York: Broadway, 2011, p. 89.
3. Kristin Lewis, "I Was Homeless," *Storyworks*, January 2014. www.sebring.k12.oh.us.
4. Andrea Elliott, "Finding Strength in the Bonds of Her Siblings," *New York Times*, December 9, 2013. www.nytimes.com.
5. Maria Fabian and Fred Smith, *Invisible Innocence: My Story as a Homeless Youth*. Seattle: CreateSpace, 2013, p. 89.

Chapter 1: A Vulnerable Population

6. Quoted in Lyndsey Layton and Emma Brown, "Number of Homeless Students in U.S. Has Doubled Since Before the Recession," *Washington Post*, September 14, 2015. www.washingtonpost.com.
7. Christensen and Denfeld, *Ask Me Why I Hurt*, p. 83.
8. Quoted in Anderson Cooper, *360 Degrees*, CNN, August 23, 2007. www.cnn.com.
9. National Alliance to End Homelessness, "A Q&A on Youth Homelessness," November 1, 2013. www.endhomelessness.org.
10. National Alliance to End Homelessness, "A Q&A on Youth Homelessness."
11. Gary Levine, "Homelessness and Poverty in America: Stats Adding to the Confusion," *Naples Herald*, August 17, 2015. http://naplesherald.com.
12. Quoted in Andrea Elliott, "Girl in the Shadows: Dasani's Homeless Life," *New York Times*, December 9, 2013. www.nytimes.com.

13. Quoted in Lewis, "I Was Homeless."
14. Quoted in Rebecca Elliott, "Fort Bend Seeing More Homeless Young People," Homeless Youth Network, February 1, 2015. http://homelessyouthnetwork.org.
15. Ann Brenoff, "7 Things About Homeless Kids You Probably Didn't Know," *Huffington Post*, May 25, 2014. www.huffing tonpost.com.
16. Andrea Elliott, "A Future Rests on a Fragile Foundation," *New York Times*, December 9, 2013. www.nytimes.com.
17. Ellen L. Bassuk, Carmela J. DeCandia, Corey Anne Beach, and Fred Berman, *America's Youngest Outcasts*. Waltham, MA: National Center on Family Homelessness, 2014, p. 10.

Chapter 2: Finding Food and Shelter
18. Quoted in Christensen and Denfeld, *Ask Me Why I Hurt*, p. 35.
19. Fabian and Smith, *Invisible Innocence*, p. 63.
20. William, "I, Too, Am One of the Estimated 22,000 Homeless Children in New York."
21. Quoted in Ben Spurr, "Five Homeless Youth Share Their Stories," *Toronto Star*, October 19, 2015. www.thestar.com.
22. Quoted in Julie Weingarden Dubin, "Mom Story: I Was Homeless with Three Young Kids," SheKnows, May 8, 2012. www .sheknows.com.
23. Quoted in Lewis, "I Was Homeless."
24. Quoted in Johnny Dodd, "Daring to Care," *People*, October 13, 2008. www.people.com.
25. Christensen and Denfeld, *Ask Me Why I Hurt*, p. 33.
26. Quoted in Christensen and Denfeld, *Ask Me Why I Hurt*, p. 88.
27. Fabian and Smith, *Invisible Innocence*, p. 8.

Chapter 3: Staying Safe and Healthy
28. Quoted in Christensen and Denfeld, *Ask Me Why I Hurt*, p. 98.
29. Quoted in Elliott, "A Future Rests on a Fragile Foundation."
30. Kevin Ryan and Tina Kelley, *Almost Home: Helping Kids Move from Homelessness to Hope*. Hoboken, NJ: Wiley, 2012, pp. 53–54.

31. Quoted in Denis Hamill, "Death of 4-Year-Old Boy Reveals Rat-Infested, City-Funded Homeless Shelter," *New York Daily News*, May 1, 2014. www.nydailynews.com.

32. Nancy Badertscher, "TB Real Concern at Atlanta Homeless Shelter," *Atlanta Journal-Constitution*, August 19, 2015. www.politifact.com.

33. Christensen and Denfeld, *Ask Me Why I Hurt*, p. 55.

34. Quoted in Dodd, "Daring to Care."

35. Wayne, personal communication with author, October 23, 2015.

36. Quoted in Lisette Hilton, "Mobile Clinic to the Rescue," *Contemporary Pediatrics*, April 1, 2015. http://contemporarype diatrics.modernmedicine.com.

37. Quoted in Rick Tardiff, "The New Face of Homelessness or Jess' Story," Shaw House, 2015. www.theshawhouse.org.

Chapter 4: Getting an Education

38. Quoted in *Athens (GA) Banner-Herald*, "More Kids in Schools Homeless," January 29, 2007. http://onlineathens.com.

39. Quoted in Nikita Stewart, "A Daunting Trip to School for Some Homeless Children," *New York Times*, November 13, 2015. www.nytimes.com.

40. Quoted in Nate Robson, "In Oklahoma Schools, Record Numbers of Homeless Children," Oklahoma Watch, May 29, 2015. http://oklahomawatch.org.

41. Quoted in Stewart, "A Daunting Trip to School for Some Homeless Children."

42. Quoted in *Athens (GA) Banner-Herald*, "More Kids in Schools Homeless."

43. Quoted in Layton and Brown, "Number of Homeless Students in U.S. Has Doubled Since Before the Recession."

44. William, "I, Too, Am One of the Estimated 22,000 Homeless Children in New York."

45. Robson, "In Oklahoma Schools, Record Numbers of Homeless Children."

46. Fabian and Smith, *Invisible Innocence*, p. 63.

47. Brenoff, "7 Things About Homeless Kids You Probably Didn't Know."
48. Quoted in Alexandra Pannoni, "Homeless High Schoolers Face Barriers to Education," *U.S. News & World Report*, September 29, 2014. www.usnews.com.
49. Fabian and Smith, *Invisible Innocence*, p. 22.
50. Quoted in Stewart, "A Daunting Trip to School for Some Homeless Children."
51. Marcy, personal communication with author, December 18, 2015.

Chapter 5: Efforts to Help Homeless Youth

52. Quoted in Dana Jirauch, "Coming Full Circle: Helping the Most Vulnerable," video, Phoenix Children's Hospital Foundation, November 24, 2014. http://phoenixchildrensfoundation.org.
53. Quoted in Jirauch, "Coming Full Circle."
54. Quoted in Bridge Over Troubled Waters, "Malcolm," 2015. www.bridgeotw.org.
55. Quoted in Hannah Greenberg, "Supporting the Students," Odyssey Online, January 2, 2012. www.odysseynewsmaga zine.net.
56. Quoted in Youth on Their Own, "Monica," 2015. https://yoto .org.
57. Quoted in Monarch School, "Meet Junior," 2015. http://mon archschools.org.
58. Quoted in Monarch School, "Athletics," 2015. http://mon archschools.org.
59. Quoted in Broome Street Academy, "Messages of Hope." www.broomestreetacademy.org.
60. Wayne, personal communication.
61. Bassuk et al., *America's Youngest Outcasts*, p. 96.

Covenant House

461 Eighth Ave.
New York, NY 10001
phone: (800) 388-3888
website: www.covenanthouse.org

Covenant House is a nonprofit organization that provides food, shelter, and crisis counseling to homeless and runaway youth. It has houses in twenty-seven cities located throughout North America. The agency's website includes information on programs it offers, as well as profiles of homeless kids whose lives have been rebuilt with help from Covenant House.

National Association for the Education of Homeless Children and Youth (NAEHCY)

PO Box 26274
Minneapolis, MN 55426
phone: (866) 862-2562
fax: (763) 545-9499
e-mail: info@naehcy.org
website: www.naehcy.org

The NAEHCY is a national association dedicated to promoting educational excellence for homeless children and youth. Members of the NAEHCY include educators, school counselors, social workers, and shelter staff, among others. The association also provides scholarships annually for homeless students.

National Coalition for the Homeless

2201 P St. NW
Washington, DC 20037
phone: (202) 462-4822
e-mail: info@nationalhomeless.org
website: www.nationalhomeless.org

The National Coalition for the Homeless is a network of homeless people, advocates, service providers, and others who are dedicated to putting an end to homelessness. Its website provides information on a variety of topics, including issues of youth and LGBTQ homelessness as well as ways for youth to become advocates.

National Health Care for the Homeless Council (HCH)
PO Box 60427
Nashville, TN 37206
phone: (615) 226-2292
fax: (615) 226-1656
website: www.nhchc.org

The HCH is a network of more than ten thousand doctors, nurses, social workers, patients, and advocates who share the mission to eliminate homelessness. Its website provides information and links to help homeless people find health care services.

Safe Horizon
209 W. 125th St.
New York, NY 10027
phone: (212) 695-2220
hotline: (800) 708-6600
website: www.safehorizon.org

Established in 1978, Safe Horizon is the largest nonprofit victim services agency in the United States. It provides services to homeless youth, including street outreach, youth shelters, and a toll-free, anonymous hotline.

For Further Research

Books

Andrew Heben, *Tent City Urbanism: From Self-Organized Camps to Tiny House Villages*. Eugene, OR: Village Collaborative, 2014.

James J. O'Connell, *Stories from the Shadows: Reflections of a Street Doctor*. Boston: BHCHP Press, 2015.

Anthony D. Ross, *Homeless at Age 13 to a College Graduate: An Autobiography*. Washington, DC: Step One, 2014.

Bob Sweeney, *Homeless No More: A Solution for Families, Veterans and Shelters*. Dallas: Dallas LIFE, 2015.

Jimmy Wayne and Ken Abraham, *Walk to Beautiful: The Power of Love and a Homeless Kid Who Found the Way*. Nashville: Nelson, 2015.

Cheryl Zlotnick, ed., *Children Living in Transition: Helping Homeless and Foster Care Children and Families*. New York: Columbia University Press, 2014.

Internet Sources

Quinn French, "Youths' Homeless Problem Won't Be Solved with Old Formulas," *San Francisco Chronicle*, September 17, 2015. www.sfgate.com/opinion/article/Youths-homeless-problem-won -t-be-solved-with-6512549.php.

Alex Morris, "The Forsaken: A Rising Number of Homeless Gay Teens Are Being Cast Out by Religious Families," *Rolling Stone*, September 3, 2014. www.rollingstone.com/culture/features/the -forsaken-a-rising-number-of-homeless-gay-teens-are-being-cast -out-by-religious-families-20140903.

Craig Phillips, "Homeless but Not Hopeless: Homeless Youth in America," *Independent Lens* (blog), PBS, April 9, 2015. www .pbs.org/independentlens/blog/homeless-but-not-hopeless -homeless-youth-in-america.

Morgan Zalot and Vince Lattanzio, "Fighting for a Place to Call Home: The Silent Epidemic of Youth Homelessness," NBC 10 Philadelphia, 2015. www.nbcphiladelphia.com/news/local/Fighting -for-a-Home-The-Silent-Epidemic-of-Youth-Homelessness-332 250942.html.

Websites

Homeless Youth Network (http://homelessyouthnetwork.org). Located in the Houston, Texas, area, the Homeless Youth Network assists homeless and runaway youth by providing housing and other support services to help homeless youth achieve independent living.

National Center on Family Homelessness (www.familyhome lessness.org). This authority on homelessness published the report *America's Youngest Outcasts*, which ranks the fifty states on how well they are addressing issues of child homelessness.

The Homestretch (www.homestretchdoc.com). This site contains information on the documentary *The Homestretch*, produced and directed by Anne de Mare and Kirsten Kelly, which features interviews with three homeless Chicago teens and strives to dispel common stereotypes about homeless youth.

TheOnlyFredSmith.com (www.theonlyfredsmith.com). This is the website of homeless youth advocate Fred Smith, producer and director of the documentaries *The Kids in the Shadows* and *The Invisible Youth of America*. It provides information on these films as well as books written by Smith.

Index

hygiene and clothing issues and, **49**, 49–50

schools expressly for homeless, 59–61

See also under effects

effects

  behavioral, 18–19, 51–52, **52**

  educational

    behavioral problems, 51–52

    being held back, 48

    difficulties doing homework, 47–48

    difficulties focusing on schoolwork, 46–48

    dropping out, 53

    frequent changing of schools, 43

    loss of earning potential as adults, 19

    poor academic performance, 44, 48

    poor attendance, 43–46

    ridicule from other students, 48–50

  emotional, 15–17

  long-term, 17–19

Elliott, Andrea, 6, 19

embarrassment, 16

emotional effects, 15–17

Fabian, Maria

  behavioral problems, 51–52

  on hidden homeless youth, 7

  on living conditions, 22–23, 30–31

  teacher who helped, 61

families

  abandonment by, 10–11, 23, 50, 63

  abuse from or conflict with, 10–11

  dysfunction, 10

  in shelters, 20–21, 24–25

fires, 37

First Friendship Family Shelter (San Francisco, California), 20–21

Florida, 15

food, **28**, 28–31

friendships, 16–17

GATES Transitional Living Program (Tampa, Florida), 57

Georgia, 15, 37, 58

Goehring, Evan, 16

Great Recession (2008–2009), 9

Haag, Tamara, 43, 47

Hawaii, 13

health

  absence of insurance, 42

  chronic illnesses, 39–41, **40**

  clinics, 54–55, **56**

  compromised immune systems, 17, 34

  difficulties finding care, 38–39

  emotional and behavioral problems, 18–19

  higher risk of

    respiratory and ear infections, 34–35

    serious illnesses, 17, **36**, 36–37

    unusual conditions, 39

  inability to have good hygiene, 34, 48, 50

"homeless capital," 15

Homeless Education Program (HEP) of Clarke County School District (Athens, Georgia), 58

homelessness, defined, 8–9

Homeless Youth Network (Houston, Texas), 56

Houston, Texas, 56

hygiene, 34, 48, 50

Illinois, 15

immune systems, 17, 34

individual dysfunction, as cause, 10

Internet access, 47

Jackson, Miss (teacher who helped Maria Fabian), 61

Katz, Lenore, 58

Kelly, Jim, 41

Kentucky, 15

Kolton, Sheryl, 62

75

Picture Credits

Cover: Depositphotos

6: Depositphotos

10: Shutterstock.com/Monkey Business Images

14: Maury Aaseng

17: iStockphoto.com/PeopleImages

23: Associated Press

34: © Bob Rowan/Progressive Image/Corbis

28: Associated Press

35: iStockphoto.com/RapidEye

36: Thinkstock Images

40: Depositphotos

45: Depositphotos

49: © Mike Brown/Zuma Press/Corbis

52: Thinkstock Images

56: © Greg Smith/Corbis

59: Marcin Szczepanski/Zuma Press/Newscom

62: Embry/Zuma Press/Newscom

About the Author

Cherese Cartlidge holds a bachelor's degree in psychology and a master's degree in education. She is a freelance editor and the author of more than twenty books for children and young adults.